I SING HIM

I SING HIM

He Gave Me Psalms

ERNEST T. DAVIS II, TH.D., PH.D.

I Sing Him

Copyright © 2016, 2nd Edition © 2018 by Ernest T. Davis II, Th.D., Ph.D. All rights reserved.

No part of this publication may be reproduced, stored in a retrieval system or transmitted in any way by any means, electronic, mechanical, photocopy, recording or otherwise without permission of the author except as provided by USA copyright law.

Scripture quotations are taken from the *Holy Bible, King James Version,* Cambridge, 1769. Used by permission. All rights reserved.

This book is designed to provide accurate and authoritative information with regard to the subject matter covered. His information is given with the understanding that neither the author nor publisher is engaged in rendering legal, professional advice.

The opinions expressed by the author are his thoughts and not to be doctrine or dogma for anyone.

Cover design by Timothy Palmer

ISBN: 978-0-9964988-4-5

All quotations in this work are from the King James Version of the Bible.

I Sing Him

(He Gave Me Psalms)

Ernest T. Davis II, Th. D., Ph.D.

Introduction

Growing up in a Christian household there are a few things that you must remember and practice regardless of the denominational background. You must remember to say your grace before indulging in meals or possibly extract the wrath of parental correction. You must remember the two most important Christian holidays associated with church goers; Christmas and Easter; both are considered occasions for dressing up with high fashion. And, you must above all memorize and know what is so commonly referred to as the Lord's Prayer; The "Our Father" Recitation. And if there is one psalm that you must know it is to know Psalm 23 in its entirety regardless of whether there is understanding or not. You must know that the Lord is our Shepherd and we shall not ever want!

This was no different in my family where the religious training and understanding was relegated to others that often had varying and often incorrect foundational doctrine, only oral traditions and recitations. But, after years of rote repetition and mindless mutterings, a light came on concerning various songs written by David and others as recorded in the books of Psalms. I say this because what we consider one book is actually divided into five parts.

It took me foremost accepting the Lord spoken of as my personal Lord and Savior to be able and embark on the journey of revelation. Only then did the psalms begin to pique my interest. The Who, what, when where and why began to form concerning these pericope of Scripture. Did David just write these because they sounded like popular songs for his day? Or, was he really relaying a message in them; even prophetic messages. Each passing year more revelation and illumination was given concerning the hymn book of David and passed down to us.

As the beginning of the revelation began to unfold, I recall telephoning my mother to speak of the Shepherd's love and guidance even in dire situations and circumstances. She thought I had gone onto the fanatical side of "church" as she had stated times before choosing to stay in the safe Sunday school pew as many often do. Yet, she listened and even asked a couple of questions. I am convinced that deep inside a religiously programmed mind is a bright light and flicker of fire waiting to be released by any means necessary and often with just a quick blow of air from the Holy Spirit. And, there are also those who will put the fire out themselves in order to not be convicted of error and challenged to repent!

Some sacred cows are hard to slaughter! They are anchored in such a way as to attempt to be eternal fixtures. Either way, there is a necessity of development that has to be reckoned with either by acceptance of truth or totally rejecting the knowledge and risking the consequences of Hosea 4:6; the complete verse. My mother was one of these people that had accepted what the preacher or others said even if it was in error. Only in her later years would she begin to discuss the Word of God with an awakened desire to have His revelation. They were wondrous times although not as many as I would have loved to have had. And, it was the Word of God that brought about much healing in both of our lives. It actually began to be a joy to have her ask questions and we both dig for the answers together. She would bring a passage to memory that I may not have discovered and vice versa! She began to find and understand God's grace and that He wasn't waiting to bring down the roof on our souls. And, no doubt Psalm 23 was the first one that we delved into on numerous occasions. So, I will make this a reflective journey in selected psalms. Let us reflect on the questions that may give us a different outlook every time we read the Books of Psalms. Selah.

Dedicated to Rosa M. Davis-McLeod, a woman who experienced much, was healed even more and deposited the hunger in me to dig even deeper into the Word of God. Rejoice in His presence eternally.

To Bennie and Ellen Dunn, surrogate parents that can never be described. While Pop Dunn is the epitome of the fashionable gardener, Momma Dunn is the traveling fish fryer. Much love to you both.

Pop Benny Dunn, you are now in our future. Your melodic voice is now singing in Him. He gave us Psalms through you. Now, you can sing to Him from us. Rest in Him for eternity.

I sing hymns to Him. Yet, I want to sing Him as in His essence and presence; engulfed by Him. Therefore, as I sing Him, all hymns remain here in this realm while I sing Him in Him. Selah.

Ernest T. Davis II

The Shepherd Psalm

No doubt the most recognized psalm written in the Old Testament is Psalm 23; the Shepherd Psalm. While prophetic and soothing, it is resoundingly recited possibly millions upon millions of times daily. David captured such imagery in his psalm until we must step back and begin viewing it with natural and spiritual eyes.

I can honestly say that I have observed shepherds in my life and how they interacted with the flock. It was amazing to see how the sheep followed the shepherd and would not follow another person or animal. They were locked onto the shepherd and that was the end of the story!

Knowing that David spent such time with the sheep, I am sure he knew each one's characteristics and even temperament. God allowed him to use this psalm to describe how the Lord deals with us! It's awesome in my eyes to see how we can truly be like sheep. And, sheep are not dumb animals as many would think.

Psalm 23

The Shepherd Psalm

THIS HAS TO BE PERSONAL

"The Lord is my shepherd; I shall not want." Psalm 23:1

I desired so much to know God in such a way that it was often painful as a youth growing up. While the circumstances of my hunger may have been far from ideal, the hunger was intense nonetheless. Often I was ridiculed by those closest to me because of this desire. Only later in life as I encountered other people with vocations of faith did I begin to somewhat understand that it was possible to know God in a more intimate way. It was quite some time before I could understand the personal aspect of embracing God. If a person is not ready to be personal, then it may be a while before they will become intimate in the sense that is necessary.

It was a very long time of development before I became personal with God in such a way as to be able to say with conviction that He was MY shepherd. We often speak in a rote manner of such things because that is what we were taught to do. But, to embrace the words of David in such a way as to understand his emotions while singing them brings a new dimension. David was such a powerful worshipper for the fact that he didn't just believe what he was saying, he lived it.

The Lord was his shepherd. The declaration was three dimensional. In heaven, David was declaring that God was his personal and undisputed Shepherd in the spirit realm. He relegated himself to being a sheep, not even lead sheep. All of the angels knew that David identified the Lord to be the Shepherd of his life to lead him in all that was to be. This heavenly declaration alerted the spiritual realm where other spirits dwell that there was to be no mistake of Who was the Shepherd for this man on earth. Everywhere in the spirit realm the truth that God was the Shepherd of David was known.

The declaration was made in the earth to the other two dimensions; soul and body. David spoke to his soul; the seat of his mind, will, intellect, imaginations and emotions. He informed his soul that God was his Shepherd and that there would not be any deviation discussion or debate of the matter. Then he spoke to his body; the earth suit. The body must come under submission to the truth that God was his Shepherd. Therefore, the body was subject to the leading and direction of Him; even enduring the rod if necessary.

David declared that he would not want for anything because the Shepherd provides all. There are times that we make pseudo declarations concerning the Lord as being our Shepherd. Yet, when the leading or correction doesn't look like we desire, then we tend to deviate from the submission that we declare. He is our Shepherd until it may look like the grazing is not what we desire or the path being taken is not what we expected. So, we renegotiate the declaration in our own minds and attempt to make it acceptable to God as if He was forcing us to do this anyway. Yet, I wonder if we were ever sheep since we choose to renegotiate. Why? Because sheep don't negotiate; they follow. Even though one may stray at a point, they ultimately remain a sheep and the Shepherd is still the shepherd.

So, in essence the beginning of submission like David is to declare boldly, "The Lord is my Shepherd, I shall not want!" Once this declaration is given and adhered to with all diligence, then we can begin our walk in the shadow. Until this declaration is given with all sincerity and submission at best we are following the sheep in front of us not knowing if there is a Shepherd. Lift up your voice. Declare. Now begin to follow His leading.

CLOSING YOUR EYES TO SEE THE PSALM

As often as I have read Psalm 23 I have never really looked at it in a prophetic manner until recently. There are times when God will reveal things to us because there is a reward in our diligence of seeking Him. I confess. I did not initially like the ridicule when a "nugget" would be revealed and fellow Christians would mock the treasure or my expression of the rhema that just dropped. I battled rejection stemming from my youth and desire to know God that now had tentacles in the church fellowship. Youthful memories that wounded us often reoccur at the most inopportune times. The nature in me would wonder why they didn't see what God shows others. Then I realized something. They were not yet ready to grasp that nugget that God entrusts with various people. It never made them bad people, but different. And, I concluded that they must have a nugget or two that I could feast on as well; if they were ready or courageous enough to share them. So as I kept my nugget, I began to see what they were willing to impart, often to supplement the treasure I received from the Lord.

When I read the Word of God, immediately I ask Him to enlighten me in this passage and to show me Christ.

Sometimes, it's instantaneous. Other times it may take some studying, digging and constant comparison. For years we were told to recite Psalm 23 with its six verses in our environment. Yet, there was no special revelation to me until recently. I asked God to show me His presence there. Well, I received more than just God as Father. I also began to see God, the Son and Holy Spirit. I am aware that some may not agree. And, truly I am well with the reality of disagreement yet still in fellowship.

I began looking at the end of the Psalm; dwelling in the house of the Lord forever. That is the destination of the journey; His house and presence! God the Father has opened His house up for my habitation! I am going to live in His house in His presence. We should use our Godly imagination to place the reality of the Word of God in our lives. How would His house look? What furniture if any would be there if any there would be any other than the table? What fragrance would be in the atmosphere? How bright would it be? I could amuse myself in hours of questions; even as a grown man! But, I would dwell in His house as the final destination of this journey through the shadow.

God the Father has had a table prepared for me in the presence of my enemies! Now how would He do that?

Would He invite all of my enemies just to sit on the outskirts and watch? Wow! He would do this for me? Again, my imagination could be active for hours and not fully grasp the reality of this image! Perhaps some of the enemies would get two invitations! I assure you that I am still in the category of redeemed even though I had this thought! But, I am confessing this is part of my imagination during my process of making a mental image. And, then I come back to spiritual reality knowing that I should not keep enemies, but bless them. But, at the moment, I kept them as enemies just for the sake of invitation and imagery.

For the complete journey, the Shepherd, Jesus the Christ, is leading me through to the end. He has made me lie down by still waters. He restored my soul (mind, will, intellect, imagination and emotions). Our minds need restoration. The more trauma of any level that we endure prior to accepting the Lord as our Lord and Savior the more we will need healing in our souls. Since our subconscious keeps a record of everything we see, hear, touch, smell and taste then we have a data bank that rivals any internet cloud of today. Even when we are sleep and dreaming often about events of the day, that "file" is expanding at exponential rates. God must restore our soul!

And, He led me through the valley of the shadow of death. It's dangerous to allow others to provide the image instead of seeking God's wisdom and artistry. Too often the valley was portrayed as something hideous; bad. I actually began viewing it as a necessary change in mountain top experiences! We can never have another mountain top experience without a valley of transition. Therefore, we should have more valleys than mountain tops. It's in the valleys that we grow. The valleys provide the nutrients necessary for the root system to dig deep. Roots cannot dig as deep into rocks as they can in the soil found in the valley. We need valleys.

It's in the valley of the shadow of death where we begin to know that something is blocking the light; alas the shadow. But, unless we know the Light Giver, we cannot understand the barrier. Yet, in the shadow of the barrier we still are aware of the Source. Therefore, as we traverse the valley of the shadow of death we will fear no evil. We know that our Shepherd or Son of the Living God is with us. We know that His rod (correction and protection) and staff (guidance and comfort) are there with Him and ultimately for our good. Admittedly, I had a problem with this concept not because of God, but because of the error in doctrine that was presented to me concerning this. There will never

be any protection, instruction or guidance without first allowing the correction of the rod. Yet, we wish to have it all peaches and cream; never having to receive any correction. This is a false mentality of today's believer.
But, in the end we see an interesting presentation of the Holy Spirit or Comforter; goodness and mercy. God in the form of the Person of the Holy Spirit is following us! Goodness is a wonderful representation of heaven or the spiritual realm. Mercy is a perfect representation of His operation in the earth concerning me. Both functions and attributes are following us all the days of our life until I dwell in the house of the Lord! Selah.

LIE DOWN AND BE LED

"He maketh me lie down in green pastures. He leadeth me besides still waters." Psalm 23:2

There are times when we need to just lie down and rest. We are moving at such a pace as to distract us from general life! The Shepherd makes us lie down like sheep in green pastures; those places of soft refreshment and feeding. If we have our way, we can lie down in things that will cause our wool (growth) to be full of stones and other things that decrease the value of our covering. Therefore, the Shepherd has to lead us to the place of refreshment then make us lie down until we realize we are in that place. Once we realize we are in that place it is then that we can appreciate the place where He has told us to lie down.

As we lie in that place of green pastures we can begin to search our minds to find out why we feel the need to move and run. It is here were we face the wolf of our minds and emotions. It is here were we begin to think through what our journey with the Shepherd has already produced. We cannot give thought to this until we learn the art of rest. We can rest, yet not be at rest. It is the added component of viewing the Shepherd standing over us that gives us true rest; no cares in the world for this time.

Now, we are prepared to move besides still waters. Fresh water is a necessity for sheep. There is need for a continuous watering of the sheep. Water is a symbol for the Word of the Lord and growth. As He leads us beside the still water, we are partakers of the fresh growth that only He can provide.

Observing shepherds and their flocks in Germany I saw them literally run from rushing water. While walking beside still water they were calm. Yet, if there was a gurgling and rushing they found their way to the shepherd quickly. It is this reason that the Shepherd leads us besides still waters; so we can drink and be refreshed without the stress of fear in the environment. From His vantage point, the Shepherd can see while we are lying down in green pastures how long we need to rest to get to the next watering point. The water must be clean and still. It must not be rushing and having all kinds of debris in it.

So, we rejoice in His leading. We gain a comfortable place in the green pastures where I can feast and rest without matting my wool. Green pastures are also a place of safety from enemies; where the Shepherd can see afar off for our safety. We have nothing but total refreshment because the next place He leads us is by still waters.

We can drink of what is needed to refresh us for the continued journey that awaits us. Oh how much does the Shepherd love us in the preparation to continue on our journey in life! He knows that we will go through valleys and are in dire need of preparation each time. Allow Him to make us lie down in green pastures. Then allow Him to lead us beside the still waters to refresh us for the journey ahead that we know not of. Selah.

RESTORING RIGHTEOUSNESS

"He restoreth my soul; He leadeth me in the paths of righteousness for His name's sake." Psalm 23:3

As we travel through life there are numerous instances when our minds become by various reasons distracted, infected or confused. Our thought pattern doesn't display the level of intellect that we are capable of. Our wills to do the right thing or perform as we should is not as resolved. Imaginations tend to run away with the slightest opened door. Even our emotions don't reflect stability. Yet all of these aspects are components of our soul.

Our soul is restored constantly by the Shepherd along this walk. Times of refreshing punctuate our lives marked by periods of fatigue form a linear map of our travels. He is the one that restores our soul because all refreshment lies in Him. Our restoration is manifested in many forms. We all are in need of refreshment prior to our journey through the shadows of the valley. It is a point of training; preparation.

His leading through the refreshed times directs us in the path of righteousness. His name is at stake. Nothing can ever make us righteous. Therefore, as we are with Him in travel the Shepherd cannot ever lead unrighteousness to the table that is being set. He refreshes us then proceeds to lead us in the path of righteousness for His name's sake. Why is His name so important? Because, it is His name that gives us full access to the location and meal being prepared. He must be righteous to enter the house of the Lord. It is His name that qualifies us to begin the valley experience. And, it is His name that brings us all restoration. We must always be able to call on the name of the Shepherd in our journey. Selah.

NEVER FEAR THE VALLEY

"Yea, though I walk through the valley of the shadow of death, I will fear no evil: for thou art with me; they rod and staff they comfort me." Psalm 23:4

As a youth I was always told that the valley was this mean and dark place where demons were waiting to take full advantage of your weaknesses. As parents, leaders and teachers, we must understand that our words have power whether good or bad. Sadly, concepts such as the dark valley are repeated over and over again until finally someone decides to stand up and ask questions. Eventually, that was me. I decided to research valleys. Yet, in my day there were no internet search engines. I used the mighty written and heavy encyclopedia; filled with images to show me.

One thing that I noticed about the valley is that it was full of vegetation and life. While there is a time of the day when darkness falls, for the most part it is light. This is not to say that no danger is lurking. Yet, it makes it much easier to spot it if one maneuvers the valley during the light. Yet, when I pondered Psalm 23 and the valley of the shadow of death, I could see that in order for a shadow to be present there must be a stronger light. It's amazing how we can gain clarity on Biblical examples by what could be considered by extreme religious people worldly examples.

I gained my perspective on the shadow in the valley by observing squirrels. Yes, squirrels helped me gain a theological perspective. I watched a family of squirrels multiply and grow. The youngest ones finally left the nest and were scurrying about in playful bliss. All of a sudden a shadow appeared. It was a hawk. They became motionless on the tree trunk. Even the mother was motionless and made no sound. When the shadow passed by the babies scurried to mother and they didn't venture far from her. That example of a shadow is what made me look at natural examples of the valley of the shadow of death; it's only temporary. The shadow passes and is always fueled by a light casting rays on something. The Light of God cast His rays on the enemy and creates a shadow. However, the enemy would like you to believe that his shadow has power. It doesn't.

Prophetically, our valleys consist of the same components as David's. His valley consisted of failed attentiveness and preferential treatment. While he failed to be attentive to the rape of his daughter and the punishment of her perpetrator a block to the light that covers a healthy valley began to form. A shadow of transgression and iniquity began to form. It began to cast an ugly shape on those traveling through the valley in that the possibility of fear moved in an eerie fashion. The lush vegetation of the valley now form sinister shapes and move in such creepy patterns in the distortion of shadow.

It is only when we move the person, place, thing or situation that blocks the perfect Light and Illumination that we can understand and enjoy the importance and purpose of the valley. It's in the valleys that we grow! We can be on the mountaintop for limited amounts of time. Yet, the air is thin. Not much vegetation grows there. Animal life is limited. But, you do have a wonderful view and able to cast vision well beyond your present place of position. Then you must return to the valley to transition and grow.

So, when the valley is upon you with all the shadows and eerie movements associated with refracted light, rejoice! It's in the valley where you grow. Begin picking provisions and drinking the water that has come from the mountainous on high fountain. Listen to God sing to you in the form of birds; call to you in the form of animals. Realize that there is a form of safety in the valley that cannot be experienced on the mountaintop.

Then realize that it is a primary growth experience the Shepherd deems necessary for you. And, finally, change your view of the current situation. View your valley experience as you just changing mountains. You can never change mountains without valley experiences.

THE NEED FOR OVERFLOW

"Thou preparest a table before me in the presence of mine enemies: thou anointest my head with oil; my cup runneth over." Psalm 23:5

I am convinced that we live beneath the intended blessings of God out of inexperience in our faith. We see the surrounding people in an area that we wish to be and immediately say that it cannot be for us. Surely with all the enemies in the region we cannot settle, function and prosper there. Yet, God tells us that He can and will prepare a table for us right in the presence of those selfsame enemies. This in logical sense is unimaginable. How in the world do you prosper in the presence of those who want your head? The simple answer is that you don't. Yet, God causes it to happen. Otherwise you will not prosper in their presence, you will die.

When a table is prepared there are many items placed on it in specific order. The covering or table cloth is a normally of fine linen; a material of multiple purposes. The utensils are made of the finest precious metals. If silver representing redemption is considered to be the finest on earth, then surely in heaven gold represents the deity of God. Not only gold but clear gold as John described in the Book of Revelation!

"And the twelve gates were twelve pearls: every several gate was of one pearl: and the street of the city was pure gold, as it were transparent glass." Revelation 21:12

Imagine the most exquisite flatware that we are humanly able to conjure up. Now, pause and think on the awesomeness of God. Could there be any way for us to understand what He would provide for us as flatware? There is no way we can even imagine such items. Yet, it is God who is preparing the table for us (me) in the presence of enemies! They are watching this preparation and knowing who it is for. You!

Not only does He prepare the table in the presence of enemies, He also anoints our head with oil! Oil, being a symbol of prosperity and the grace with mercy of God, being placed on my head, symbolizing my thoughts and emotions, is a powerful symbolism. God has touched our minds with prosperity in that we will prosper even in a hostile environment! His anointing reminds us continually of His mercy and grace. He has freely given them to us by virtue of relationship, not entitlement. We so ignorantly attempt to qualify ourselves for His mercy and grace, not understanding that we will never be entitled to it by any means.

Before we move on, let us look at what has already transpired. God is preparing a table for me, personally, in the presence of my enemies. Those who sought to do me harm and even kill me are forced to watch the preparation of a table by the hands of God that is specifically for me! God has not dispatched angels to accomplish this. He is doing this by Himself.

Now my head is covered with His oil, not the oil of man. The Hebrew word is *dshnth* (תנשד). It literally translates to "you make sleek". God, with His personal heavenly oil is making sleek my head (the symbol of my mind, will, intellect, imaginations and emotions) with His anointing. I have had to stop many times to attempt to imagine this. Yet, I cannot! God is making me sleek with His special oil in the presence of my enemies! I won't even be able to focus on the enemies because I will be overtaken by His presence! So, everything that I thought was challenging means nothing at this point. I am made sleek with the oil of God sitting at the table that He has prepared. The valley was nothing compared to this! I repent for having whined and complained in the valley.

My cup is running over! The cup is a symbol of your personal life, responsibility or provision. In all of these examples, it runs over! My life is abundant and running over into other lives. My responsibility has been increased and running over that I may delegate to others. I can't perform all the responsibilities that He has given to me. Yet, He has given me others to carry on the functions and responsibilities that are ultimately mine.

His provisions are running over in my life and responsibilities. I have no need for anything since He has poured it into my cup (life or responsibilities) and it is overflowing. There are times when I hear the God is the God of more than enough. While I understand clichés and slogans, I try to ponder how if we can define "more than enough" unless we can effectively define enough. We can't truly define enough because we can't define sufficient. If we attempt to define sufficient we must define a timeframe of provision. No one can provide the timeframe of provision because time belongs to God. So in that timeframe, how would we know what would be enough in order to define what would be more than enough unless we are omniscient? We cannot! So, when clichés or slogans are quoted I must pull my mind away from them. Otherwise, I end up with a headache attempting in a feeble manner to ascribe understanding to an illogical God.

But, my cup runs over. The Source pours into my life and overwhelms the space or capacity to contain what is being poured in me. The example given in the word *runneth* gives the connotation that has filled and continuously running over; satiation. I am being satiated with the blessings of God to allow them to run over into the earth to others. Can you imagine (this is a feeble attempt at understanding) being a water hose with a heavenly water running through you to the earth? What would the hose, being the conduit, feel as this is occurring? I'm not sure which would be able to handle the continuous flow of God blessing the complete world through my little vessel apart from His grace given to me allowing me to do it! Either way, I will never say that it is enough when it comes to God blessing me. Fill me up Lord until I overflow! Selah.

LOOSING EVERYTHING BEFORE DINNER

David had issues in his life. He had many. Yet, God said this was a man after His own heart. I often heard this mouthed and recited, yet void of any revelation and explanation. As with many things that were "churched" (the language of Christianese) we just spoke things out of those before us speaking them as the cliché of the day. This was no different. How was it that David could be a man after God's own heart, yet suffer so many shortcomings and maladies? I believe it is because David wanted to be so knit with God that regardless of how he was down, he was constantly looking up and toward the Object and Person of his affection and praise.

Absalom, the son of David, had such a disdain for his father until he wanted to overthrow him with a vengeance. He felt betrayed by David on many instances. In no way was he to allow this to not be avenged by his own actions. Absalom actually did briefly overthrow his father's rule all because of what was in his heart; pride, anger, revenge and unforgiveness.

Too often children think they have all the answers and wise authority. In reality, they may have some answers concerning things. However, God has established a mandate to "honor" your father and mother. It is one of the Ten Commandments; a commandment with promise! I would be naïve or just ignorant to say that all children have things to cherish their parents for. It just doesn't happen, especially in today's world. However, all people are to "honor" their parents. One of the definitions of honor is to "confer" distinction upon.

In the instance of David, he didn't make a decision concerning a crime which upset his son Absalom. Arguments on both sides could be offered. Therefore there is no need at this point to debate the issue. Absalom was just upset that things didn't work out the way he desired. It is a sad situation in modern times where the respect of son toward father as well as father toward son is absent. Such is the case here with Absalom. The third born son of the King is now being the first rate pain in his side.

David didn't extract punishment for the rape of Absalom's sister, Tamar. This caused such bitterness until Absalom harbored such bitterness reaching deep and becoming a root of bitterness digging deeper and deeper into hatred. Bitterness is a poison that can infect even the most loving person if not identified and extracted! While arguments or reasoning can be made for all aspects of this account, Absalom felt that his sister was not vindicated by his father, nor did he think his father even cared. No doubt, he knew that the advice to violate his sister came apart from his father. And, it wasn't just an inside job which upset him even more. And, now, there is no emotion toward Tamar, his sister.

Yet, the Word of God records that David wept for his son every day (2 Samuel 13:27) without making mention of his daughter who was relegated to live in the house of her brother after being sexually assaulted. So often we will only view one aspect of something that while visible and even known to be a transgression will only be a small aspect of the complete remedy. So, just as with an infection, if not treated and eradicated to the root, it will return in other ways that are often more deadly and damaging than the initial malady. Such was the case for Absalom.

Pastor Anthony Wallace provided us with an analogy concerning "church hurt" of which I examined my past wounds. It was profound. He stated, *"Church hurt is overrated. It happens because the person didn't vaccinate and inoculate themselves against the germs of sin and offense from those in the congregation. It's much like if you don't vaccinate yourself against disease you will become susceptible to infection. This is the*

same in offense. If you don't vaccinate and inoculate yourself with the Word of God on a regular basis when the disease of offense is present you become infected because of your own refusal to take proper precaution."
I am convicted of this. Whether it was by ignorance or sloth, every time I had been offended and wounded in a church was because of this example. While there are times when the inflictor of the offense has responsibility toward the well-being of the oft times young saint, ultimately we have to be the ones to take the Biblical medicine.

I recall a person that wanted to be a deeply loving person. Yet, there was a hidden bitterness from a trauma of childhood among numerous others that had taken root. Regardless of the outward appearance of success and stability, there was such a hideous bitterness that too many times gave entrance for hate to seep through; ready to injure others because they could not identify the point of their pain. Then there was the denial, justification or justified ownership of it. Nothing can justify the ownership of sustained bitterness and hatred of any person; nothing! Yet, when bitterness is released, it touches more than just the carrier of it. This can be contagious as well. While others around them held them in esteem and even high honor, should anyone not agree with them experienced havoc and banishment;

even a snort of ridicule followed by warped lies to attempt to assassinate the person's reputation and character.

On a sidebar, your reputation is given by man and may be assassinated. However, your character is of God and toward Him and can never be assassinated by man. Yet, the bitterness was sustained in life by the memory, not existence or life, of the event and culprit.

When you focus on a person, place or thing constantly, you will without doubt let it consume your sub-existence and therefore your present thoughts. All it takes is for a name, resemblance or any other trigger to release it all over again which is a perception. It doesn't even have to be true. Only a perception can trigger the painful poison that will spew into your soul. I would like to submit as well that perhaps there are other areas of ones memories that deserve the same if not more of the disdain that has been funneled into one subject if we are to be fair. Where there is such poison of action fueled by bitterness and hate, there is a trail of other infections that infected numerous others of which confession must be made and forgiveness received.

This is the same as Absalom. Even after the death of Amnon, the brother that caused all of offense with his actions, that same bitterness thrived and caused the usurping of power concerning King David; his father. How powerful is such a hate and bitterness that the son of the king would begin to overthrow his own father in such a way that had it not been for divine intervention would have succeeded? Nothing is more powerful than love. But, hate can sure pack a punch placed in the wrong hands and fed by the frailty of man's mind!

DOUBLE COVERAGE

"Surely, goodness and mercy shall follow me all the days of my life; and I will dwell in the house of the Lord forever." Psalm 23:6

There was a time in Germany when I would just sit and watch the shepherds as they herded sheep through various pastures. I loved the way everything seemed to flow like water. There wasn't much the shepherd had to do but walk to the destination if he had a good sheepdog. I learned the value of the sheepdogs when he didn't even have to look over his shoulder or voice a command. The dogs kept the formation tight and mobile. This is the same as in our walk as sheep through the shadow. We are kept tight by goodness and mercy; the expression of sheepdogs that keep us tight and mobile.

I pondered why David would use two identities or attributes to follow us since this was a shepherd's description. I know there must be a prophetic reason for such a description. As I mused upon this, I could imagine that Goodness and Mercy were attributes of God expressed by the operation of the Holy Spirit. These attributes and functions continually keep us in line with the Shepherd so that He won't have to look back to see where we are. And, if there is danger, they will alert the Shepherd for protection.

Goodness is the attribute expressed in the entire heavenly or spiritual realm. Everything in the presence of God is perfect; lacking nothing. The worship, the praise, the atmosphere and the fellowship is all good! We would not experience anything that is not of a perfect nature. Yet, we need a touch of that goodness here. This is where the Holy Spirit follows us that we may continue in the paths of righteousness; goodness..

Mercy is God's operation toward us in this sinful world. He showed mercy before the foundation of the world when the Lamb was slain (Revelation 13:8). Mercy operates daily for us from the Lord. His mercies not only endure forever, but are renewed towards us daily. These two attributes follow us, guiding us constantly.

So, in this Psalm I can witness the Godhead in fullness. I witness the Father preparing the table for me in the presence of my enemies. They will watch as I feast on what is prepared. They will see Him anoint my head with oil and my cup running over. I witness the Son as the Shepherd leading me besides still waters, making me rest in green pastures full of comfort. He is even leading me through the valley of the shadow of death and comforting me with His rod and staff. Never once has he allowed anything to be neglected. Why? He has it all covered by Goodness and Mercy representing the Holy Spirit; the Comforter. He is in the rear ensuring that nothing will harm me or allow me to go astray. He will nip at my heels to keep me focused on the Shepherd. Such a wonderful example given by David could only be revealed by God!

This is even a Messianic psalm as well! Jesus had to go through the valley of the shadow in order to get to the house of the Lord where He will dwell with His bride forever. His table will be prepared for Him in the presence of His enemies. His cup runs over because of all that God has imparted to Him. And, His church, Goodness and Mercy, shall follow Him all the days of His life bringing the Gospel to the world. We are not goodness and mercy to a world hungry for Christ. I'm just amazed at how God revealed so much to David. Selah.

CLOSING THE GAP (GOODNESS AND MERCY)

On a few occasions I have had the opportunity to observe flocks of sheep and their interaction with the shepherd. It's wonderful to see how they are not scattered about. All of them tend to want to be very close to the shepherd especially if there is a perceived danger. They act like children getting close to parents! While there are always the ones that will attempt to stray, the majority of them will be close to the shepherd.

On the other hand, there were the sheep dogs that ensured that they were in very close proximity to the shepherd. They tirelessly ran back and forth, barking and nipping at the heels of the sheep to ensure they were in line. No sheep could get behind the dogs! I loved watching the dogs work. When the sheep rested, they rested. When the shepherd moved, they went into action herding the sheep.

This is what happens as the Shepherd is leading us through the valley; Goodness and Mercy are in action ensuring that we are in close proximity to the Shepherd. There are times when we are close but not very close. In the example of Peter as recorded in Matthew 26:58, he was close to Jesus but yet following from afar. John on the other hand was always close to Him; leaning on His bosom at the table, following Him close even as He went to the cross. We have two individuals but a different dimension of closeness. This is where we must evaluate our walk. How close are we to Him? Are we close enough to the Shepherd where Goodness and Mercy won't nip at our hind parts?

Our ability to maintain safety and hear the voice of the Shepherd is conducive to the closeness we share with Him. Sheep are not necessarily like cattle in huge herds. They tend to be in smaller units and closer. Cattle roam. It's just that simple. They will roam. Sheep tend to stay in close proximity to the shepherd. This is our example in our traveling through the valley. We must stay in very close proximity to Him. When we close the gap, He will ensure that Goodness and Mercy never let a threat sneak up on us. Why? It is because these two also protect us from those threats that attempt to harm us hidden from our view. Selah.

ADDITIONAL MUSINGS OF PSALM 23

THE FOUNDATION OF FAMILIAL LUST

So very often we have things occurring in the family that are hideous actions regardless of what way you view it. Such was the case with Amnon and Tamar. Tamar was a beautiful young woman who was also the half-sister to her rapist. Yet, Amnon allowed himself to become vexed and worked up over her beauty instead of maintaining familial respect in accordance with the Law of Moses. This all begins because of outside influence toward a familial situation that needed to be addressed.

It is a shame how often we will listen to outside voices to deal with a spiritual problem. Yet, we will not seek wise counsel in the House of God. Please do not embrace what I am not saying. There are just as many voices in the House of God that spew idiotic wisdom as well as those who speak wisdom from above. This is where our dependence upon the Holy Spirit grasps our need. We must operate in discernment! While some answers or remedies may even make sense, only God's wisdom given to us will be the necessary answer to navigate the situation at hand. Such was the case with Amnon.

Amnon was the son of the King. This gave him privileges that could only be imagined by others. Not only this, but he was the first-born of his father which entitled him to the double portion. Sadly, a generational mistake was in the making. Rueben slept with his father's wife or concubine so did Amnon heading down the same path. While Rueben slept with his father's concubine, Amnon took it another step to sleep with his half-sister. He crossed the line of understanding just as his ancestor which would open the door for dissention and a shifting of family and destiny family members.

Throughout the Body of Christ violation occurs when lines are crossed for the sake of immediate gratification causing eternal consequences. I say this in all truth because often these transgressions are subtle in their beginnings. We as leaders must be vigilant to the warning signs. While the initiation can come from either direction, it is normally the more stable person or someone in leadership capacity that has the perceived power to influence the victim's action or inaction.

Amnon embraced the advice of Jonadab, his cousin, that surely didn't have the morals of the family; especially the royal family. He voiced his lust, desire and instant gratification. Therefore he gave it such a life as to become a life that would do anything to be preserved. He devised a plot to feed his starving hunger of lust. And, Amnon carried it out with precision. I can see why

Absalom was livid seeking justice! When such precision is given into an action, it leads a person to wonder if secretly Jonadab wanted to be the abuser and since he couldn't he decided to pour gasoline on the lustful fire of Amnon to allow him to be a surrogate for the fantasy. This is just a thought that I have concerning this.

Yet, on another thought, I wonder how much David really knew of his own children. In modern times there can be a disconnection if there are other attention stealing activities of the father. David was an international statesman, military officer and prophet after all. Did the King notice the inordinate attention being shown to his daughter? Did he question the sickness of his son or offer to provide another solution to comfort his ailing son? There are so many questions that could be answered in the backdrop of this passage until many volumes could be written concerning them.

But in this case the desire that became so strong that even cultural mores were not enough. It is the same as when one commits a sin, it goes well beyond the person and the victim in all cases. This is where the upheaval went well beyond just the act.

First of all, it involves God Whom we have transgressed against, then the person or people on earth, and very often many of their descendants! There is never a sin that only touches one person. David very well knew this. Bathsheba was his lustful downfall that involved the same characteristics of this account including murder. And, now his son would begin to fall to the sin of murder caused by anger and a need to avenge the honor or his sister.

I have viewed many things in family trees that one could follow at some level through the succeeding generations. Even in my own family tree there were things that continued through. Yet, with the power of Christ the curses are broken and the blessings intensified. We pass more than curses. We also pass blessings. Many don't speak of these. Remember, we inherited the knowledge of good and evil, not just evil.

It is imperative that we recognize all things that are contrary to God's word and plan in our bloodlines. Otherwise we will surely allow things to enter into the gates of inheritance that will hinder our destiny and the destinies of others in our lineage.

THE MINDSET OF THE VALLEY

As we look at the mindset of the valley, we see past points and points to reminisce. David can look back at this and grasp memories to begin to write. Now, Absalom is attempting to overthrow him and also destroy him due to perceived injustice and inaction concerning his daughter and Absalom's sister. Yet, in all of this, David looks back and emphatically states for the present "the Lord is MY Shepherd, I shall NOT want" (Psalm 23:1).

Interestingly enough the Hebrew language has only two tenses (past and present/future) compared to the English language with three (past, present, and future). The past tense is considered the perfect tense. While I have no reference point for my mindset concerning the following statement, I would like to think that everything in the past is perfect because it all belongs to God. He has made it perfect because He had Paul record in Romans 8:28 that "all things work together for good for those that love God and are the called according to His purpose". So, David took a brief trip into his memory and concluded that God was and always would be his Shepherd. He reasoned within himself that he would not want in any form no matter what things appeared to be.

Perhaps I am one of dramatic thought and a vivid imagination. So, here is where my mind travels when I read this powerful psalm that is also a Messianic promise. David has memories no doubt on his own shortcomings and transgressions. He recalls the consequence in which the sword would not depart from his house according to what the Lord spoke to him as a consequence of his transgression. Now, here he is remembering how he was the one that sent Tamar to her brother not knowing that she was in danger. He was lacking as a father and leader in this aspect. And, now his third son is looking for revenge for his sister against their own father.

Surely a parent will not harm their child unless totally necessary and no other option exists. And, even then there still may be a level of restraint that could be deadly for either party. Therefore, there must have been some restraint given to the actions of David in order to not harm Absalom; in just eliminating him totally. After all, he was a skilled and accomplished warrior! So many thoughts were going through David's head. Yet he stilled his mind in order to worship and listen for God's voice. He began to speak from his spirit; the seat of his relationship with God.

REHEARSING THE PAST LIFE AND FUTURE PROMISE

David began rehearsing what was to take place. There was the first thought. The Lord *IS* (present tense) *MY* (personal ownership) Shepherd. His thoughts brought the memory of his life as a shepherd and what it meant. He was constantly concerned about his sheep. They were treasured almost as one would treasure another human. He made the Lord a present (is) positional fixture in his existence and also a personal (my) not general Shepherd. Just as the sheep looked to David as a person and present shepherd at one time, he also looked to God. It is at this point that we must mirror David.

There was a time in my life that I had no other option but to rehearse just as David did. My brother had died by suicide on Easter Sunday. We had been making plans to enjoy a vacation together. I sensed something was wrong based on what he was talking to me about during my morning and evening commutes; ministering and praying for and with him. He even received the Lord into his heart and confessed that Jesus Christ was Lord. You see, there is a hidden nugget in the order in which Jesus and Christ are listed in Scripture. If Jesus Christ is listed, then Jesus is in the place of deliverer while Christ will later come for development. If it is listed as Christ Jesus the Christ is in the primary function as developer as Jesus has already delivered them. Search the Scriptures. We may or may not agree. At this time my brother accepted Jesus and had not yet allowed him to be the Christ to develop him.

Then on that fateful Easter Sunday, I received a call that just placed me in a numb place; disbelief. Immediately, I adamantly confessed and declared that the Lord is my Shepherd. Immediately, I ran to my Shepherd for His comfort. I received the peace and comfort to get me through that situation. Yet, as I was able to minister to other family members and friends, I was also being comforted by my confession and declaration. Then, the heat really got hot.

My brother was the youngest of my mother's children and shared her birthday. While I often thought (then later knew) that he was her special young one, I watched my mother take his death in a terrible way. Her baby boy had died by suicide. There was anger and hostilities as many were blamed for his demise. Even I wondered at times, who was to "blame" for pushing him over the proverbial edge? Sibling rumors pointed to various sources. But, as I reminisced over the many things that he was troubled about, no one person or thing was the source of his pain. It was many sources that weighed heavy on him. Therefore, I had to return to the Word in order to remain grounded; and the Lord was indeed my Shepherd for where I ran for all that was needed especially comfort. My promise was to his widow to ensure she was cared for even if there was to be no other contact by any other family member during that time. While even she was a source of blame to many, it was not her. It was my brother's desire to leave in a permanent solution to a temporary situation; he didn't want to go through the valley of the shadow of death. He got stuck looking at the shadow.

My mother was heartbroken. She began to visit relatives and speak quite often to me telephonically. Her grandsons, my brother's sons, still came to stay and travel with her in the early part of the summer; June and early July. And then something happened. She began to tell me things that she had harbored for what seemed like an eternity; her pain, shortcomings and lost desires. Some of these confessions were quite awkward and concerned me in such a way that I may never release them to others; especially family! But, one thing I do realize retrospectively is that my mother was beginning to walk into the shadows; that dark place where there was the shadow of death.

There was such a love and peace that had come upon her as if she knew that it was only a place of transition. We had discussed the Greek word; *agape*. While initially she didn't understand the concept as I explained other Greek words for love and showed her that *agape* was only attributed to God, she understood! I remember telling her that agape is the most painful word in the Bible. It will always cost you everything but the other person nothing. I still live out that reality many times over today.

She had been hospitalized the week before and released on the Monday prior to her passing. I took vacation from work and was to see her that day as well; Wednesday. She promised to reveal something to me when I arrived at her house that day. While sitting at a lunch, I received the called that she was going back to the hospital by ambulance from her live in companion. I left my plate there and drove like a maniac to arrive on time. About thirty minutes into the drive I called back for an update. This time she answered the phone. She was a little livid; thinking a neighbor had called to tell on her to me. Yet, it was her household companion that alerted me. She assured me that she was going to be alright now that she had spoken to me. She was going downstairs to wait for the ambulance and would see me when I got there. I was a little lost in thought as to what she meant. The moment I hung up the phone, I realized that she was not going to make it. She was preparing to transition due to her grief.

Within two minutes I received a call from her companion, hysterical with noises of resuscitation in the background. She wasn't responding. Mother had gone to sit in her favorite barrel back chair (of which is still in my study to this day) and transitioned home to the Lord.

In retrospect I can see that she may have very well waited for me to arrive since they kept resuscitating her until close to my arrival. When I walked in and viewed her body, she was still very warm. Yet, instead of grief and pain, I felt a peace and determination. I declared that the enemy had not won. And, I would carry the Gospel like madman intent on destroying the kingdom of darkness. First my beloved younger brother of whom we shared a special relationship had departed. Now, my mother, although wounded and full of secrets had departed. I'm glad that she did release some secrets to me which brought me into more understanding of the why in my upbringing many things were so painful to me. With the release of some of the secrets forgiveness was given and received.

Too often, we view difficulties as an attack from the enemy. At times I beg to differ. Paul told Timothy in 2 Timothy 3:12, *"Yea, and all that will live godly in Christ Jesus shall suffer persecution."* So, what we consider as an attack is really the assigned opposition to your destiny. In order for there to be an attack, there has to be a home base; a headquarters of sort of which to launch. Since the enemy is already defeated, this territory is not his. So, he has no home base unless one wishes to give him a diplomatic mission in the Kingdom of the Earth with diplomatic immunity. And, in this place he has "diplomatic immunity" of which he can wreak havoc then claim immunity and not be prosecuted. Not so!

Opposition on the other hand describes what happens when advances are made such as to retake what is rightfully ours. When we are ensuring that the gates of hell will not prevail against us, we are encountering opposition from the squatter on the earth; the enemy. So, this opposition is nothing more than the pushing back on a victorious advance ensured by the death, burial, resurrection and ascension of our Lord and Savior, Jesus Christ! Yes, the enemy is opposing us! He has grown fond of his squatter landscape! But, we are advancing in the name of the Lord or Hosts!

So, my beloved, when you have to rehearse the past, it is for future assignment and promise. It is up to you to embrace it as a one in all process from God. The past is the dirt to fertilize your future. Some of us have strong fertilizer. Selah.

SAME SUBSTANCE DIFFERENT FUNCTION

There are times when we can only arrive at the intended imagery of a word in the Bible by going to the original language of which it was recorded. I enjoy it although I am in no way a Hebrew scholar. But, I find some things fascinating in just musing over the Word of God! We have the concept in Psalm 23 of the rod and staff. Both are made from wood. Both have a distinct purpose. And, both are necessary in the protection and guidance of the sheep. Yet, often this small detail is overlooked.

Wood is often prophetically categorized in a symbolization of something that can be manipulated by man; a symbol of man's effort that can be destroyed. Yet, in this instance, it is the Lord or Shepherd that has wood in His hand; the thing that symbolizes man's humanity. His rod (*sebet*) and staff (*mishenah*) comforts us!

I have described the Hebrew language to those that think it is simple as the most simplistically beautiful and complex language in the universe. I don't say that in jest either. To my knowledge every word has a root of three consonants. So, in the word *sebet* the root word gives the connotation of an unused root. This is interesting. I speak this because the root being unused is now being used for correction and protection. So, there must be a reason that the rod is listed first in this pericope of Scripture. The rod, correction and protection of what has not been used as a root, must come first. Then we can proceed to guidance of the staff.

Next, we understand the staff; *mishenah*. While on occasion it has been translated to mean a stave or spear of sort, in this translation and many others it describes a staff or something of firm support of all kinds. I got so excited in reading these nuggets and imagining what the Shepherd was doing! He uses the unused root (*sebet*) of the tree the produced our present support of the staff (*mishenah*) and used them both to comfort us in our journey through the valley! God chastises those that He loves! In other words to dispel the ogre mentality often incorrectly attributed to our Father, He chastises (teaches through correction) us because he loves us with a rod. Then He supports everything that is given to us with the staff. All of this is occurring as we are going through the valley of an altered course; the place where we have directed ourselves due to our own action or inaction.

The carnal mindset would be to view these two pieces of wood as sticks that will cause discomfort. While one may cause some discomfort, it also provides needed protection from predators and enemies. While they may not come from the exact same tree, I am sure there is a distinct possibility that they may. The root is underground; the intentions of the tree in forming the rod which is to be foundational correction. Then the staff which is above the ground; that which provides strength and stability. It provides the needed balance in our function and existence.

I challenge the reader to no longer just view words on the pages of the Bible, but to look at other aspects of the recorded word of God. See what words are in what order. See, which word is first. Challenge yourself to push to the original language and view that particular word within the context of the Scripture. It's the little things that take us further yet produce the biggest reward. Selah.

IN THE FACE OF MY ENEMIES

The table of the Lord begins being set under the shadow of darkness in the valley. Ironically, someone can see what is being done even while in the darkness. Your enemies can see in the dark. Does that surprise you? It shouldn't. Why? It shouldn't bother you because traps are set in an environment of darkness; whether natural or spiritual.

While in the military we were trained to develop our "night vision". This is where your eyes adjust to very low light and gives you a measure of visibility. It's like when you are sleep and wake up. You can actually see in the dark until you turn on a light. Then your night vision leaves. In the dark is where enemies hide. It's here where God sees what is going on while leading you through the valley. Not only does He see what's happening, He begins to prepare a table for you as your enemy looks on.

I often looked at this verse (v:5) in wonder. The progression of thought of the song takes me from walking through the valley and not being afraid to the rod and staff comforting me to setting the table. All of this is being accomplished while in the valley of the shadow of death. Imagine in your kitchen with a burglar hiding and you begin setting the table knowing he is there hiding. This is where my imagination is taken with how God is with me in the valley of the shadow. I don't need night vision because I am trusting in His vision which surely surpasses anything that I may see.

There is nothing mentioned in this verse that I must do but trust Him. He prepares the table in the presence (middle) of my enemies. God sets the table with everything that is needed; furniture, linens, seating, utensils and food! All of this is occurring while I actively trust Him in the valley. He anoints my head with oil! I again cannot see in this valley. I am under a shadow that is hindering my sight. But, I am feeling the oil on my head while in the valley's darkness. Yet, all of this is occurring simultaneously as I am following the Shepherd. So, instead of being concerned with the darkness enjoy what is in the shadows: Him. He is preparing the table, anointing your head and being the joy of the journey.

Since we may not be able to see anyway, then we may as well close our eyes and experience the table being set and feel the oil dripping over our heads. Imagine in knowing what will be on the table; food that cannot be imagined in its goodness. Imagine the oil used to anoint our heads; a heavenly mix beyond fragrance and consistency. Then as we imagine all of this, know that even our imagination cannot come close to the reality of what He is doing in the shadows. Even with our best imagination, we will never be able to effectively conceptualize the workings of God. It is at this point of total creative and imaginative surrender that I can say He is awesome! Selah.

THE STEPS OF THE SHEPHERD

I am amazed at how an animal can tell the gait of their master or owner. I make reference to the pets that I have owned and also to one particular calf that my grandfather let me raise as much as possible during one summer vacation. The animal can tell the sound of the steps of the owner or master. In this case the shepherd can walk and the sheep know his approach or steps.

I would like to amuse you with the story of my calf; Butch. My grandfather gave me the responsibility of caring for a calf that he purchased for his farm. I was responsible for the feeding, brushing and washing of him. This was my calf. What little urbanite could boast that they owned a true farm animal; but not in the city. Once Butch learned my approaching gait he would meet me eagerly at the gate. He wouldn't do this with other humans. I quickly fell head over heels in love with this animal. He was my escape from the hard work of a farm; something I was in no way used to nor wished to continue.

I returned home to the city longing to see my calf again. In November we returned to my grandfather's home for the Thanksgiving holiday. I bolted from the car straight to the pen where my calf was kept. He didn't come to the gate. I called and called. Still no Butch bounced around the corner. So, I went in the pen and investigated. There was still no Butch to be found. I went to my grandfather for answers. Where was my prized calf now grown into a steer no doubt? His answer has possibly scarred me concerning farm animals even to this day. He sucked his teeth and began to give an account. "Well, part of him is in the oven for dinner, part of him is upstairs in the freezer and another part of him went up with Aunt Betty to New Jersey", he said. I was devastated. Needless to say I didn't eat any dinner and limited my culinary intake for the whole holiday. And, to top it off my mean and uncaring countrified cousins would mock me by opening the oven or freezer and call out, "Butch, Butch"!

My point is that just as Butch knew my gait and could identify it from others walking at the same time. The sheep know shepherd's gait. They can follow it during the times of shadowy uncertainty. They are close enough to hear his footsteps and be secure that he is in control of their destiny and journey.

In Genesis 3:8 we have a record that Adam heard the voice of the Lord walking in the cool of the day. Since this was post-fall could it have been that there was a measure of darkness that was experienced? There was a shadow of impending death over him in the Garden. Yet, he heard the Lord's voice in His gait coming to him. It's a wonderful analogy; the voice of the Lord came walking! Perhaps this will shed more light for the reader of the journey through the valley of the shadow of death. Just quiet your soul and listen for the voice of the Lord walking with a gait. Remember, you are on your way to the table that is being set in the presence of every enemy that has vexed you. Just listen for His voice and steps and follow closely. Selah.

Psalm 37

Promises of Future Blessings

Often I have been led to read Psalm 37 for various reasons. It could have been because of mistreatment, guidance or reassurance. It's all there. I love how David asks God why things are happening concerning the evildoer. His observation is that the evildoer is prospering and he's upset! Yet, God is letting him know that it is all noted. I have often felt the very same way!

I recall one of the first times I personally read Psalm 37. I had heard it quoted and expounded on in various verses. But, I had never read it for myself in its entirety. This time reading it the very first verse arrested me. I was being falsely accused by someone in a warped sense of manipulation. I knew it was all a form of control. Yet, it could potentially be damaging. So as I was lead to read the Bible, I stopped on Psalm 37. The very first verse spoke to me in such a way as to bring peace upon my complete residence.

"Fret not thyself because of evildoers, neither be thou envious against the workers of iniquity. For they shall soon be cut down like the grass, and wither as the green herb." Psalm 37:1,2

I realized that I didn't have to be worried about the evildoer! I didn't have to be "caught up in my feelings" about how they were prospering in this dishonesty. God promised in one sweeping touch that they would be cut down like the grass and wither up. They would not prosper. They would be removed.

At that time I had matured from praying prayers such as "God, kill them". I had cried out to God concerning me. I wondered why it was that I was walking in His direction, yet these people were coming to discredit and lie on me. I just cried out asking if this was the will of the Father. Immediately, I was led back to the same two verses and felt the peace again.

As normal the enemy will send a messenger. Immediately the phone rang with someone who had "heard" what was supposedly happening. I remember I began speaking the verse that God just gave me and a stern warning that if they wished to be a part of what had already happened then they could keep talking. (I didn't know at the time what I spoke of what had already happened to the person.)

I didn't hear from the person for quite some time; six weeks to be exact. Then when I did I learned that the very day that I spoke to them the individual that was so deceitful and dishonest suffered a heart attack. They didn't die which was a relief to me. No one should rejoice in the misfortune of another no matter what wrong they did to you. They are also the creation of God who Jesus also died for. And, certainly there should be no joy in a person dying without knowing the salvation in Jesus Christ.

That news actually scared me. I spoke that God would cut them down just as He said. And, He did. That drove me again into the Psalm to see what else was there. Until that time, I had only meditated on the pericope that He gave me; verses one and two.

Trust in the Lord and do good; so shalt thou dwell in the land, and verily thou shalt be fed. Psalm 37:3

There is that word again: trust. Trust in the Lord. And while you are trusting prove that you are by doing good in your time of trusting! So while I am trusting that God will vindicate me, I am to do good to all people as well. This was a point of direct concentration for me. The old man had to die. As I was raised, if someone wronged you, then you wouldn't do anything good for them in ANY fashion. Some even have gone so far as to speak of hideous things to do to someone if they needed help. Yet, here is God. He is spoken of so much as to being the Force behind a lot of things. Yet, this is completely opposite what I had heard in this psalm from other verses. Many people would only pick out certain verses to justify actions. And, surely this wasn't one of them. To grasp the full psalm in its entirety causes one to become humble quickly.

Often times I have heard verse four quoted as a catch all/bless me verse. Oh, what danger lies ahead when you separate a verse for human understanding apart from the rest of the Scripture! A very base understanding would be that if I enjoy the things of church worship then God is obliged to give me the things of my heart. I had this mindset at one time. *Oh horrors!* I even tried to convince God of my revelation for Him to get with my program! Words cannot explain the idiotic mentality that I possessed by seeking a humanistic understanding instead of a heavenly revelation.

Delight thyself also in the Lord; and He shall give thee the desires of thine heart. Commit thy way unto the Lord: trust also in Him and He shall bring it to pass.
Psalm 37:4,5

The key to this verse is its inclusion in the complete psalm. While there is merit in God's word as individual verses, it can never be extracted for personal gain or selective interpretation. I delighted myself in HIM, not just the activities directed at Him. And, in turn He gave me the desires to PUT in my heart which was of His mind and will! Instead of me looking and saying I wanted what I saw, He put his desires for me to recognize it when I saw it. Then as in verse five I had to trust in God, not my own ability in order for HIM to bring it to pass. That was a wonderful thing. Why? It was because I had something to compare it to; my own ignorance.

It didn't happen instantaneously even though it could very well have understanding Who God is. But, it took some time; development on my part to receive it. This is where the next verses come into the process.

And, He shall bring forth thy righteousness as the light, and thy judgement as the noonday. REST in the Lord, and wait PATIENTLY, for Him; fret not thyself because of him who prospereth in his way, because eof the man who bringeth wicked device to pass (Psalm 37:6,7)

We must remember, David was watching the wicked. While we must apply God's word to all aspects of our lives, never forget the context in which David was writing. He knew the wicked were busy. He knew that it was being allowed at that time by God. So, he asked God a question. He didn't question God. He just asked Him a question. And, God so graciously answered him.

God in essence told David to just relax; wait for it. Don't worry about what you see happening when people are doing evil and making evil schemes in the open. Just wait for it. When it comes, you will surely see how it drops out of nowhere!

Cease from anger, and forsake wrath; fret not thyself in any wise to do evil. Psalm 37:8

Don't get all out of sorts and angry. Don't throw any tantrums. And, surely don't let your mouth utter anything that may be regretted. Our words can forfeit the righteous judgement and deliverance of God. In transparency, I have witnessed this in my personal life. I was wronged in such a way as to have to bring a lawsuit against the organization. It was a sizeable award to be possessed. Yet, because of my mouth and words of disrespect uttered, I had to drop it as instructed by the Lord. I had to be righteous and just drop the lawsuit because I wasn't patient in waiting for God to do what He does. I wanted to put my two cents in. And, that two cents cost me the loss of thousands of dollars. We must be quiet. Let the move of God speak, not us.

For evildoers shall be cut off: but those that wait upon the Lord, they shall inherit the earth. For yet a little while and the wicked shall not be; yea, thou shalt diligently consider his place, and it shall not be. But the meek shall inherit the earth, and shall delight themselves in the abundance of peace. (Psalm 37:9-11)

The promise is again that we are to wait, allowing God to be God. Yes, it sometimes doesn't look good. Nor does it feel like anything is good for us. Yet, God is always in control of every aspect of creation. I will concede that at times we process surrounding events and circumstances through human understanding. But, we must train our minds to process it from the position of God's understanding and power not our own. God said to just wait and the wicked would be no more. You will think of where he used to be, but he will no longer be there. This is a promise beyond anything we can fathom. Yet, I can fathom it if I try to (because I will never be able to fully understand it) the awesomeness of my God!

The wicked plotteth against the just, and gnasheth upon him with his teeth. The Lord shall laugh at him: for He seeth that his day is coming. The wicked have drawn out the sword, and have bent their bow to cast down the poor and needy, and to slay such as be of upright conversation. Their sword shall enter into their own heart, and their bows shall be broken.
(Psalm 37:12-15)

There have been many instances, although I often didn't recognize them immediately, where this pericope rang true. I watched those who were overcome with wickedness just have such a disdain for those who were of upright conversation or life. They were so angry at poor and needy of any culture or civilization until they wanted to wipe them out if not literally then culturally. Yet, God is true to His word.

When Jesus said that the poor would be with us always, He didn't intend for anyone to try and wipe them out from the face of the earth or out of culture. He allowed this for us to always have an opportunity to show love as God has shown us love. So, we must be very careful that we don't allow the culture of today to tell us that any group of people regardless of culture needs to be the scapegoat for our perceived maladies. If we do not remember anything else, remember that the Jews were once this group of disdain. And, you see how God loves His chosen. Selah.

A little bit that a righteous man hath is better than the riches of many wicked. For the arms of the wicked shall be broken; but the Lord upholdeth the righteous. (Psalm 37:16,17)

While I grew up not in such a prosperous and affluent home, I had sufficient as to not starve or sleep on the floor. Yet, society bombarded me with images of "success" and comfort. I heard stories of my parents and how they had nothing compared to what we had. We were not poor in a sense, but poor with a poverty mentality and existence caused by many factors. So, off I went into society by way of the military to begin collecting those things that I saw others of ill repute and wicked actions possessing. My very first paychecks from Uncle Sam's Army (the United States Army) produced a wardrobe that had me dressing as sharp as a razor. Yet, I hadn't been able to get shoes as sharp as my garments. So, initially my clothes were fashionable, but my shoes were still military issue until I could get to a shoe merchant. As soon as I got to the shoe store, I made a beeline home on a quick leave in between assignments. All of the compliments I received on my attire had me thinking I had arrived! It was validation. Little did anyone know; I had only a few dollars in my wallet. It was expensive to put on such a display without the funds necessary to maintain it. And on the pay of a private you can only make so much happen.

Years later after trying to maintain this lifestyle until it took me down into a spiral of destructive behavior and substance abuse, I began to appreciate small things. I wish to be clear that substance abuse does not mean addiction as often used synonymously by others. I became thankful. I detoured away from that wickedness that society placed in front of me. Am I saying that all fashion and abundance is wicked? In no way am I saying that. I am not fashionable and have abundance. Yet, my mindset and heart is much different in that God is first in my life.

I began to appreciate things in another way. Once I lost everything that I deemed important, then I could actually see God. It was at that point that I began to understand what was truly important. He was the Source that provided all things. Everything else was a "re" source. I was so at peace with what was considered a little bit compared to earlier times in my life. It was as if I was in a Joseph development. I went from having so much to having nothing then to having it all once I understood God. Even at this time in my life, whatever was lost was not lost. None of this is mine anyway! This is all God's! As He allows me to steward over His possession, I am pleased to just be counted worthy.

In another writing of Psalm 119:71 it speaks *"It was good for me that I have been afflicted, that I may learn thy statutes."* Anyone in that has in retrospect viewed affliction can deduct wisdom and development from it. I don't care if it was the loss of a house, job or income. We can deduct some form of wisdom was derived. But, the most powerful wisdom that is a result of it speaks to learning the statutes of the Lord. During these times of affliction I have seen the hand of the Lord in them although many times it was in retrospect. I treasure them as wisdom to be handed down.

My brother-in-law and I were once sitting on the porch watching a mentally challenged man walk up the street with his lunchbox. This man who was mentally challenged cleaned the building in which I worked. Daily I would watch him about his duties with such joy; even singing sometimes. Yet, here we were, skilled and highly paid employees that always had issues. Yet, here this man comes, limited in mental function but as happy as could be.

As we watched him walk up the street, the question was posed. Did he really know happiness? Or was he limited to never understand happiness? My answer to the inquiry was something that sparked an hour long conversation border lining debate that attracted others that were enjoying the evening. My answer was simple. Could it be that his limitation allowed him to know true happiness with what little he was perceived as having? And, could it be that we have "evolved" into perpetual discontent due to our desire to have it all? After all, God did say that a little that a righteous (a man in Him) man have is better than the riches of many wicked. Again, this is no theological or spiritual pitch for poverty or for limiting one's mental ability. But, the spirit of poverty can rest on a billionaire if he allows it. Selah.

I speak this because of travels in areas of missions. I have observed many that by Western standards are poor in many ways; poverty stricken. Yet, their faith was powerful and their joy was complete. I learned so much from them as to be content with where I am. While I must admit it would not be my desire to live as such, I realized that while we had possessions they had peace. And, the longer I stayed with them, the more I understood it. Even now that I have returned to my home their memory is etched into my mind.

God promised that the arms of the wicked shall be broken. When that occurs, how will they continually grasp those things they deem as important and needed?

It will be like bobbing for apples with your mouth taped shut! Yet in the same verse, God promises that He will uphold us. It has been my experience that I couldn't hold myself up. I can never do what He always does.

The Lord knoweth the days of the upright; and their inheritance shall be forever. They shall not be ashamed in the evil time; and the days of famine they shall be satisfied. But the wicked shall perish and the enemies of the Lord shall be as the fat of lambs; they shall consume; into smoke shall they consume away. (Psalm 37:18-20)

God has promised that he remembers us as His righteousness in Christ Jesus. He knows our days and our inheritance which will be forever in Him. When evil comes, we are never ashamed. In days of famine we are satisfied. Such promises are beyond awesome! We tend to get our news from various media sources. I tend to look around and go to the main Source.

There have been times of famine of sorts in my life. Yet, there has never been a famine of the bread of life; His word. And, as long as there is never a famine of the word there is always hope in the promises of the Word.

God promises that the wicked shall perish and be as the fat of lambs. The fat of lambs gives the illustration of lamb fat on a hot fire. It melts and falls on the fire causing it to get hotter. So, as the wicked continue their activities, this is their end; burning up. Yet, in all of this, we will not be consumed. Will we have difficult times? Yes, we will. They are to be expected. But, even in the difficulties around us, we will never be consumed. We will be at peace if we allow Him to be our peace.

The wicked borroweth and payeth not again; but he righteous sheweth mercy and giveth. For such as be blessed of him shall inherit the earth; and they that be cursed of him shall be cut off. (Psalm 37:21,22)

I used to read this and obtain a very base revelation from it. The wicked borrows and doesn't pay. That was very simple. But, I never went any further than this. As I begin to dig deeper and labor in prayer for more than my mind could produce, I began to see things in a much different way.

We as a family have purposed in our hearts to never lend money. I know it sounds harsh. But, there is a method to this perceived madness. First of all, if we were to lend money according to the word of God we should never charge interest or usury on the loan (Exodus 22:25, Deuteronomy 23:19). We should never cosign for anyone (become surety for a loan) including our children (Proverbs 22:26). Therefore, we don't lend money.

If we receive a request and can assist with or provide the need, we give the money. If the person decides to repay us, fine. If not, then we are not in expectation of it. We place the burden of desire on the receiver, not us. This way there is no strain on any relationship. After all, God gave to us even though we had no means of repaying Him in the form of Jesus Christ. As God blesses us, we are to become blessings to all around us. We will inherit the earth. Others that are cursed of Him will be cut off. So, we will always be a blessing to others as much as possible as He is a blessing to us.

The steps of a good man are ordered by the Lord; and He delighted in his way. Though he fall, he shall not be utterly cast down; for the Lord upholdeth him with his hand. (Psalm 37:23,24)

It is awesome that we have the promise that God is ordering our steps. These verses in the Hebrew language paint a wonderful picture for us to understand. The Hebrew language paints the wonderful picture of God going before us ensuring our steps are in the order of His intent. The word "*kuwn*" (כּוּן) is a verb referring to God doing the action, not us. Even in the King James Version of the Bible, the word "good" is added. In the original Hebrew the word "master" is used. The Hebrew word "geber" (גֶּבֶר) denotes a mighty man. God is speaking to us that in Him we are mighty. And, in this might imparted to us, He is ordering our steps.

Even in the following verse, if we fall we are not thrown away. In the original language we are not "cast forth" or thrown away. His hand upholds us. This is awesome in that we all have fallen and will continue to fall in some fashion as we walk in this life. If there is one verse that speaks to a loving father not beating us down and kicking us out for what shortcomings we have, it is this one!

I have been young, and now am old; yet have I not seen the righteous forsaken, nor his seed begging

> ***bread. He is ever merciful, and lendeth; and his seed is blessed. (Psalm 37:25,26)***

David was reflecting on his life. He was once a young man, and now having aged he chose to reflect on an important aspect. No person that was righteous was ever forsaken by God, nor was their seed begging bread unless it was their choice. I love the promises of God because they extend generationally. His promises to me extend to my seed. And, it is a perpetual extension as my seed come to know my God for their own relationship; making Him their God.

Our seed will never beg for food or even for the bread of life! Even in the parable of the Prodigal Son which I identify, he never really begged. He had something to eat physically even though it was conducive to his behavior and surroundings. And, the word of life that he knew remained with him even in the pig pen. We can never forget what God has ordained to be placed in our spirit before the foundation of the world and reinforced on this earth.

We are to be ever merciful and lend a hand to people. Our determination to be a blessing extends beyond those in our fellowship. We are to be in the world showing them the love of God and His sovereignty by our lives. As we continually walk to do this, our seed is blessed. How are they blessed? If they are not in the way of God, then they are preserved. Their health is maintained. They have opportunities opened up because of His covenant with us. There are so many ways to be blessed that are more valuable than riches.

Depart from evil, and do good; and dwell for evermore. For the Lord loveth judgment, and forsaketh not his saints; they are preserved for ever: but the seed of the wicked shall be cut off. The righteous shall inherit the land, and dwell therein forever. The mouth of the righteous speaketh wisdom, and his tongue talketh of judgment. The law of his God is in his heart; none of his steps shall slide.(Psalm 37:27-31)

Our God is just. We often fear using the word judgment because of perceived negativity. In essence that word "judgment" is only making a distinction between something. Verse 27 God makes a distinction between his saints and other. We as the saints are preserved forever. Isn't this what He has always said? But, as He has made a focus point of this psalm, the wicked will be cut off while we as the righteous inherit the land and dwell in it forever. This is an example of the Nation of Israel. They will always dwell in that land. God promised it.

Our mouths should always speak the wisdom of God and not of this world. Our tongue should make a wise and Godly distinction between things without being judgmental in our conversation. It is when we are judgmental that we hurt ourselves and many. And, in addition, we wound those trying to get closer to God. Therefore, we will answer for such things in days to come. We should always be mindful of our speech.

The law of our God is in our heart. And, what is in our heart will surely come out of our mouth. So, there is no way we can have God in our heart and a judgmental attitude. It's impossible. God gave us righteousness through Christ. He didn't judge if we were good enough. He judged us unworthy by our sin, yet provided what was needed to redeem us to Him. And, He didn't require prequalification! As we walk in His directive, none of our steps shall slide! The law of his God is in his heart; none of his steps shall slide.

The wicked watcheth the righteous, and seeketh to slay him. The Lord will not leave him in his hand, nor condemn him when he is judged. Wait on the Lord, and keep his way, and he shall exalt thee to inherit the land: when the wicked are cut off, thou shalt see it. I have seen the wicked in great power, and spreading himself like a green bay tree. Yet he passed away, and, lo, he was not: yea, I sought him, but he could not be found. (Psalm 37:32-36)

Truth in this earth involves wicked people; period. They will look to slay you in some form. They will be ones who attack you. And, for a news flash not often thought of, wicked people attend church. So, whenever there is a thought of a person that is a member of a church doing wicked things to people, understand that all wicked need to come to Christ. Some only make it to church, and not into Him. Others are on the continual journey that we all travel. Either way, God's promises are true in and out of the church.

We have a promise of God, to not be overly concerned with the wicked. When they are cut off, we will see it. It doesn't mean that they will not have power and prestige. It only means that God allows things in order to show His power and glory. God will even allow the wicked to bring His plan to pass! Nebuchadnezzar was such a person. I marveled at how God called him His servant. For years I poured over this. And, now I understand. God uses whomever He wishes. It's that simple. And, unless we have the promises through Christ we will still be wicked and to participate in the wicked bracket for punishment. It is never God's will that any will perish. But, it is His will that we accept Christ to avoid the judgment brought about by our own decision.

As David recorded in verse 35 of the wicked growing in great power, I have also witnessed it. It was awesome, truly awesome in how they prospered. Yet, what was more awesome was how in a twinkling of the eye, they were no more when God stepped in. Never rejoice at the demise of another. Even now, I have memories of the wicked being removed and being no more. My heart does not rejoice in it; constantly wondering if they ever heeded the warning to come to Christ. My heart is especially heavy for the ones who ridiculed the Gospel that I spoke and ridiculed me for standing on it. I cringe.

Mark the perfect man, and behold the upright; for the end of that man is peace. But the transgressors shall be destroyed together; the end of the wicked shall be cut off. (Psalm 37:37, 38)

The Hebrew text gives the indication of the perfect man as being a flawless one in God. I love it. We are not flawless in ourselves. We are flawless in Him. When we find a man such as David described we are to mark him and see his end; peace. That man that understands, trusts, and follows after God has peace as his end.

I don't pretend to know how to describe this peace. I can just say that in my own life, there have been times where there should have been no way that any peace would be present. Yet, in the beginning of turmoil I went to the Lord in prayer being honest about my personal feelings. Too often we go to God to tell on another person. Why not be honest and tell God what He already knows; how you are feeling are acting? But, I spoke His promises and word. By the time I left there, I was in such a peace that was almost eerie. The situation was still there. I was still in the middle of it. Yet, there was a peace that truly surpassed all understanding. This is the end of that man that is walking in Godly perfection. It is not the end of the transgressors. Their end is to be cut off; period. Again, I reiterate to never celebrate another's demise.

But the salvation of the righteous is of the Lord: he is their strength in the time of trouble. And the Lord shall help them, and deliver them: he shall deliver them from the wicked, and save them, because they trust in him. (Psalm 37:39,40)

I was driving and meditating recently on how many Christian-based organizations and many other groups say that they supplement the Word of God to make a person better. I was perplexed on how anything that is created can add something to the creation to enhance what only the Creator can do. But, then that is me. Sometimes I do wonder about things such as this.

Our salvation is of the Lord. It is in Him that we receive any righteousness that we are imputed. And, in my time of trouble, any trouble, He alone is my strength. That trouble can be family, friends, war, financial and a malady of others. Either way, God is my strength. We must keep it very simple in our faith. God is the foundation, the focus and the enveloping Presence that we have. We must not involve anything or anyone else in the equation with God. It is all about Him.

In conclusion, if we follow His plan, Word and leading, we have a wonderful promise in verse 40. It intrigues me that the original writings didn't have verses. Yet, in the years that followed numbers were assigned to specific parts of the writings. Since there is no word for coincidence in the Hebrew language then there is no coincidence that the final verse assigned a number was the number 40; the number of testing and judgment. In this verse God promises to help us and deliver us. He promises that we are delivered from the wicked. The reason for this promise is that we trust, rely, believe, and grasp hold of His promises. This is such a wonderful thing. In all of the testing that we may experience, God has promised our end; peace. And, the peace in Him is indescribable. Selah.

Living in Hiding

Dwelling in the Secret Place of Promise

Psalm 91

Admittedly, until the last decade I never really paid much attention to Psalm 91 except for the excerpt that Satan attempted to use against Jesus Christ. Yet, even in that aspect I was amazed at how there was a promise of rescue. This is one of the most beautiful of the psalms written by David in my humble opinion. But, then again, depending on the season of my life each one may hold a special place.

I am well aware of the contention concerning authorship of this wonderful psalm. But, regardless of one's leaning to one or another, I personally believe it was penned by David. Why? There is much here that would lend to David penning it. He was so madly worshipping the Lord; just loving God. He describes things that in my own mind and meditation could only be described by a man in close proximity of the tabernacle housing the Ark of the Covenant. Am I penning this work to argue the point? No. I am simply stating why I believe the way I do. Knowing that many psalms were penned by various people, it would not matter to me if someone else was proven to have penned it. My enjoyment and blessing is in the fact that it is of God and has many promises which I embrace.

As I began to research Zion compared to other locations in the Bible, I discovered that Zion was a mountain or hill that was occupied by the Jebusites. They were a warlike people that still occupied Zion formerly known as Jebus the city. While Joshua didn't destroy all of them, but killed the king, the remainder occupied what was referred to as Jerusalem and particularly Mount Zion until the invasion of David which routed them.

David was not the first one to attempt to take Jebus or modern day Jerusalem. Others had tried at various times. Yet, he was the only one successful. The Jebusites were known to rain arrows down on those attempting to reach the citadel on Zion. Yet, David prevailed. Then David dwelt in the citadel that had evaded capture for so long. Alas, Zion became a place known for as a special place that was home to King David.

Now, all of Zion is in Jerusalem, yet all of Jerusalem is not in Zion. We may use that as an indication of the three degrees of the Tabernacle of Moses as well. Judah, Jerusalem and Zion mirror the outer court, the inner court and the Holy of Holies. It was to Zion that David had the Ark of the Covenant delivered and built a tabernacle to cover it. And, here is where I believe he penned Psalm 91 as a reflective and protection promise for all people. Zion is a place standing apart from Jerusalem; a place of intimacy and closeness. And for that purpose there is a significance in our faith as it relates to that location; a place of closeness.

He that dwelleth in the secret place of the most High shall abide under the shadow of the Almighty. I will say of the Lord, He is my refuge and my fortress: my God; in him will I trust. (Psalm 91:1,2)

The beginning of this psalm bespeaks of one dwelling in a specific and hidden place. The secret place of the Most High is a place of humility. It is in humility that a person can dwell in such a place of secrecy while being exposed to humanity.

We can walk the street clothed in humility which is invisible yet audible and visible when we speak. No one can see the humility of where we dwell; that secret place of the Most High. It is under His shadow in that secret place of humility that will prevent us from being humiliated. Either we walk in humility or be exposed in humiliation. We choose humility. Or God will allow us to be humiliated. It's simple choice.

It doesn't matter what I think. It matters what He promises. My protection is in Him. God is my refuge and my fortress. I am in the protection of Him. And, metaphorically I am not only dwelling in the City of Peace (Jerusalem), I am also dwelling above it in the citadel of Zion which is in the shadow of the Almighty. Is there a better place on earth that a person can live?

Surely he shall deliver thee from the snare of the fowler, and from the noisome pestilence. (Psalm 91:3)

I'm a city boy. I wasn't raised in the country, although I did enjoy some country visits. So, the thought of a snare took me to another place. I had to go and see what a snare was. I had to look it up. To my surprise, I had seen snares set in many ways; beginning with cartoons of my youth.

A snare is something that will trap a creature (or in this case birds) to either cage them or kill them. Well, seeing that this is in reference to the enemy, I am sure he doesn't want to cage us. He wants to totally annihilate us.

Satan is described as the fowler that sets the snare. I imagined a bird flying without any cares through the atmosphere. There is suddenly a trap that is sprung. The bird is restricted and possibly killed. This is what the enemy wishes for us. While we are soaring in the life of God, traps are set to at best maim us causing us the inability to soar and fly.

David writes that we are guaranteed safety from the snare of the fowler. The snare may be spring, but our protection is always there. Surely, He constantly is on watch for the snare that is set to inhibit our movement. I've never hunted animals with a snare. But, I am told that they are very effective; often more effective than other types of traps.

So, as long as we are in the secret place of the Most High there will never be a snare that will trap us. In this place there is no room for traps or maladies. We are in His presence. This in no way means that they are not set. It just means that we have the promise of God that He personally will protect us from the snare of the fowler. I'm thankful for His love and protection toward me.

"He shall cover thee with His feathers, and under His wings shalt thou trust. His truth shall be thy shield and buckler. Thou shalt not be afraid for the terror by night; nor for the arrow that flyeth by day; nor for the pestilence that walketh in darkness; nor for the destruction that wasteth at noonday." (Psalm 91:4-6)

In this modern time we are witnessing the fulfillment of prophecy at an alarming rate. However, we are under the feathers and wings of God for protection. As a hen will spread her wings, stiffening her feathers and pressing down to protect the chicks, God gives this scenario for us. We are under his protection from many dangers and exposures. I rejoice in seeing this.

I recall as a child being at my grandfather's farm. I wasn't much of a country boy, but I loved nature. I once saw a hawk fly overhead and swoop down to grab a rabbit trying to run for cover. So, I knew how fast they were. Then one day I saw the chickens scatter to the trees or in the chicken coop. The shadow of the hawk hit the ground. One hen had chicks with her. She clucked loudly and the chicks ran under her wings. She laid down in such a way as to have her wings and tail spread to where one could not see the chicks. I watched this protective move and was marveled by it! I waited to see if the hawk would attack. It never swooped down. It kept on flying in the direction it was going. I could see in the field where it began to dive. Yet, I couldn't see if it made a kill. Then the hen rose and clucked while running. All of the chicks followed into the hen house! This is the type of protection God gives us. He overshadows us with His protective covering until He directs us to move.

His truth that is spoken by Him is our shield and buckler. It is our defense and can even be used offensively if necessary. For this we shall not be afraid of any terror by night (those things that lurk in darkness to attack). Nor shall we be afraid for the arrows that fly by day. These arrows are blatant attacks from influenced people or spiritual attacks whether they are thoughts, words, or deeds. He protects us. A simple truth such as this should always cause courage and confidence to exude from us.

The pestilence that walks in darkness is nothing more than illnesses or disease that cannot be detected. We have had outbreaks of many illnesses that have come through darkness. Yet, God has promised us that it will not come near me at all; or my household. These maladies along with destruction that waste at noonday are things that come upon us suddenly. While some may come, we are still in Him. Therefore, no matter what happens, we are still in God through our Lord Jesus Christ. We are protected. Will some still be afflicted? Yes. But, even in that the victory is already won.

A thousand shall fall at thy side, and ten thousand at thy right hand; but it shall not come nigh thee. Only with thine eyes shalt thou behold and see the reward of the wicked. Because thou hast made the Lord, which is my refuge, even the most High, thy habitation; There shall no evil befall thee, neither shall any plague come nigh thy dwelling. For he shall give his angels charge over thee, to keep thee in all thy ways. They shall bear thee up in their hands, lest thou dash thy foot against a stone. (Psalm 91:7-12)

I imagined a thousand people falling next to me. It is unimaginable by my mind! I have seen a few people fall as if in a game or some event causing people to fall. But, a thousand people seem astronomical! Yet, not only will that one thousand fall, but ten thousand by my right hand; the prophetic indication of my own strength. Again, God has overwhelmed me with the promise of protection in Him. In his will and defense, He will give me the power and authority to literally cause ten thousand people to fall if they come against me! With such awesome power comes awesome responsibility. Nothing will come near me. Only with my eyes will I gaze upon those who wished to do me harm, seeing their reward from my Father.

This protection extends to my dwelling. I am assured that no protection from any insurance corporation will provide the protection that God can. I recall in 2011 while in prayer, I heard a specific word of the Lord. He said, "I will shake this place and send a storm." I didn't know exactly what it meant and spoke it to my pastor as the Spirit instructed me concerning this. For the next weeks I couldn't get that out of my mind! Then it came to pass.

Three weeks to the day from when the Lord spoke that word, it hit. I was living in Delaware in the United

States. First, there was an earthquake that was centered in Virginia and shook much of the east coast. I was at work when the building began to shake violently. I knew immediately that it was an earthquake. I watched as many ran out of the building. I can remember walking calmly for two reasons. The first was that I had my trust in God to care for me. The next was that I couldn't run if I wanted to because of an injury. But, I watched other men forget the unspoken rule of women and children first. I remember sensing a spiritual tone concerning this was coming, and discovered later that it was a warning for me to remember His promise. Then later in the same week we welcomed Hurricane Irene! Never in my life have I ever witnessed or even heard of an earthquake and hurricane in the same week. Then I remembered the word given in prayer three weeks prior. I actually got scared and wouldn't speak for a while until God soothed me; speaking to me that He does nothing without telling His prophets.

But, during that time my wife and I never left this area. Many were evacuating because of the hurricane and the threat of flooding. Delaware is not the highest point in America above sea level. Yet, not many floods come to this particular area. We prayed, purchased party food since those that were sticking it out had purchased everything else. We then settled in for a celebration of sorts. Don't ask me why. But, this is where we were. We confessed that it would not come near our dwelling. And, it didn't. Even the dog wasn't nervous, especially while enjoying treats from us. There were others homes that experienced damage and flooding. We didn't have as much as a shingle or piece of siding damaged. His angels kept us in all our ways. Truly they held us safely in our residence unless we would have hit our foot on the bedrock of Delaware in flooding. Many days go by where I recall and remember this, especially when the media prognosticators of doom spew their poison. It's under His wings that I trust. And, I experientially know that His angels are eager to defend and help us. Selah.

Thou shalt tread upon the lion and adder: the young lion and the dragon shalt thou trample under feet. Because he hath set his love upon me, therefore will I deliver him: I will set him on high, because he hath known my name. He shall call upon me, and I will answer him: I will be with him in trouble; I will deliver

him, and honour him. With long life will I satisfy him, and shew him my salvation. (Psalm 91:13-16)

I am promised that I will walk all upon the lion. The lion represents that loud and visible danger that we encounter in life. We have lions that make it known immediately the intent to do us harm. He has claws to rip us apart if we allow him to grasp us. And, he has fangs to tear into our flesh to devour us. Yet, we are triumphant.

And, then there is the adder. This is quiet yet deadly creature that slithers into small crevices of our watch. It packs a deadly poison; ready to latch onto us and releasing death. The adder has some very peculiar attributes. They are totally silent. Often there is not even a hiss to be heard as it is present. It never closes its eyes; forever watching. There is no need to eat daily and their sense of smell is acute. So this creature will wait until there is a perfect opportunity to kill. Often there is a beauty about it which is deceiving. But, the poison injected is fast acting and lethal. Yet, our God promised we would tread upon them!

The young lion and the dragon represent strong attacks. While the lion gives a roar that has the ability to strike fear in any person, the dragon is a mythical creature representing what is not real according to Apostle Nate Holcomb. I am amazed at how many times we fear something that is not real!

One person once told a group of veterans that the fear of something is worse that the event itself. This has rung true in my life on more than one occasion. God tells us not to have the "spirit" of fear. Yet, He never said we would not fear. As a matter of fact fear can be used as respect when used and allowed to stand within the parameters set forth by the Holy Spirit.

And, as we set our love totally upon God something wonderful occurs. God delivers us and sets us on high away from the terrestrial things that tend to distract and harm us. His deliverance extracts us from relationships, places and things that drive us to destruction. If we are not focused on God, we will focus on something. We are designed to focus our sight on something. Therefore, we need to focus on Someone! And, as we focus on Him we know Him. We know the name of God; His many names. We know that Jehovah is only a partial name without the adjective aspect connected making Him Jehovah and a function. His is Jehovah

Rapha, Jehovah Jireh, Jehovah Nice, and even in times when we are lost, Jehovah Turnaround!

My Lord has promised that when (not if) I call on Him He will be with me in trouble. It would fail me to count all the times there has been some type of trouble in my life and I called on Him. Never has He been absent from my troubles; NEVER. There were times when I may not have "felt" Him present. Nevertheless, He has always been there. It is interesting how we often do not realize that God spends so much time following us around in a sinful or backslidden state. He follows us, waits for us and then draws us to Him. Then He begins to "lead" us if we allow. What an awesome God we serve!

In all of this my wonderful Lord not only delivers us, but He also honors us. Imagine that! God delivers us from those things that are dangerous and deadly. Then He honors us after He was the Honorable One that delivered us. We were without honor. Yet, such a wonderful God honors us. An, He doesn't stop there!

God honors us and gives us long life and shows us His salvation. While we are being honored, He shows His salvation to us. In turn our long life is to show others the wondrous existence and expressions of a mighty and awesome Lord!

With promises like these, why would anyone not fall at the feet and worship such an awesome God? Selah.

www.ingramcontent.com/pod-product-compliance
Lightning Source LLC
Chambersburg PA
CBHW070434010526
44118CB00014B/2039